"What is a song without excess?" Calvin of odd odes, eddying odysseys, antsy sti various acts of kindness, cruelty, panic, ҕ _____ panted under the "standoffish stars" by Elvis and Eros, Rossini and Ceres, Billy Budd and Bobby Kennedy, the fire- and flower-tongued voice of these poems—chthonic, muscular, debonair—endeavors to overflow limits with lyric, while its elemental "song with Rogue shadows" rebuffs official national power and its tweeting twit-in-chief. Governed by thunder and lightning and birds, by a gravitas of red, *The Breathing Place* suggests that beauty may be a seismic, even cosmic disorder.

ANDREW ZAWACKI, author of *UNSUN : f/11*

Cal Bedient's poetry has always been singular and I can happily attest that the *The Breathing Place* is as sui generis as his other books. Dazzling, peculiar, piquant, *The Breathing Place* is bold and picaresque, with dashes of the Western. His kaleidoscopic play on these dark times tickles the ear, drenches the senses, and saturates the mind. I absolutely love this book and you should too.

CATHY PARK HONG, author of *Minor Feelings*
and of *Engine Empire*

At once galloping and exact, Cal Bedient's newest volume is a work of energy and invention; I found myself racing down the staircase of these poems, eager to bring each phrase-shaped wonder into view. This world is familiar in its unlikeliness and lit up by paradox, by O'Hara's erased orange hanging in the sky like the sun. Like tomorrow's sun today. It's shrewd and it's tender. It stuns me a little, and it makes me feel religious, as if I were French.

JOYELLE MCSWEENEY, author of *Toxicon and Arachne*

Cal Bedient's new book is a ruminating, visionary work, the power of which draws from a fierce attending to the element of water. "Living water" and "planetary water"—the element connecting the local mountain wilderness rivers to global rising seas—mark the passage of time where new "currents in the currents" become familiar returns from the past: "the chafing of limits in the fashion of water's pulsing pliancy." The Republic reels with white fascism and from wall-building and from withdrawal from climate accords and from lead in the water system—from all of these "millions of White Accidents" against which Cal Bedient's laments are wholly unprecedented in their primal sublimity and startling pragmatism.

RICHARD GREENFIELD, author of *Subterranean*

Teeming with utter, gem-cut particulars but vast as the "ever-more-enormous material world" itself, *The Breathing Place* titillates with radical specificity as it stretches one's perception to the limits of what it can hold. Bedient has always been drawn to what glimmers, shudders, sizzles and combusts; his poems blister with a beauty rooted in turbulence, defiance, and "the rage to be extravagant," as if each of them—even the most elegiac—were, at heart, an argument that all true poetry should emulate "the Blast that got us here in a Perfect Offense to reason." Coming to us late in history and late in the poet's own life ("at eighty-three," he writes, "I am past caring"), these new poems persist in celebrating the "furious blunder of creation," but do so with extra measures of tenderness, poise, and self-reflection, situating Bedient among the very best and boldest of our "grasshopper-quick troubadours," who still spin "cosmic splutter" into song.

TIMOTHY DONNELLY, author of *The Problem of the Many*

THE BREATHING PLACE

The Breathing Place

CAL BEDIENT

OMNIDAWN PUBLISHIING
OAKLAND, CALIFORNIA
2020

Cover image by Brian Shields, *Piano,* 2018.
Oil, Gesso, and Graphite on Canvas. 59 x 67 inches. www.brianshieldsart.com
Courtesy of Brian Shields and Michael Warren Contemporaty Gallery,
Denver, Colorado.

Library of Congress Cataloging-in-Publication Data

Names: Bedient, Calvin, author.
Title: The breathing place / Cal Bedient.
Description: Oakland, California : Omnidawn Publishing, 2020. | Summary:
    "The "breathing place" - individual, bespoken - is where the world
    enters uninvited, where "fair is only an experiment," where poetry's
    resistance has "slackened, gray, with some rain," where "the garden is a
    gulf in the intercom, where "today's word from Delphi / is delphinium,
    expensive / blue word, dust payment due tomorrow," where "seven of
    my sweet loves drove off of cliffs . . ." - in short, a place of jolts and
    wrongs, if also of opportunities: "Engage / Lower your oars for the
    recommencing." It is met here by a style of nervous immediacy, a style
    built for alertness, not comfort, ready to shove the English language
    around Americanly, as Gertrude Stein encouraged and Dickinson
    mastered, and, further, to break out of reality, that already known"
    -- Provided by publisher.
Identifiers: LCCN 2020024615 | ISBN 9781632430823 (trade paperback)
Subjects: LCGFT: Poetry.
Classification: LCC PS3552.E314 B74 2020 | DDC 811/.54--dc23
LC record available at https://lccn.loc.gov/2020024615

Published by Omnidawn Publishing, Oakland, California
www.omnidawn.com   (510) 237-5472
10 9 8 7 6 5 4 3 2 1
ISBN: 978-1-63243-082-3

CONTENTS

you must break out, she said, out of reality, but break it down
with you, down into the abyss as you fall.

Friederike Mayröcker, "Narrating of a Narratio"

I.

Limits of the Containing Air

Coupling

Sonntag is the worst, He's killed twenty-seven men,
He's matter disgusted with matter. To him,
the soul's a campfire burning in sunlight,
phantom muscular movements. Seven hours
into star-sprout, Colt gets the coffee going.
Cooper is mad clear through. But they talk
friendly, You see no sign of blood. Woman
in there is Talon. Todd Boysee named her,
The one with the missing eye. "Where you groin?"
She'll ask any man comes along. As for the veteran
Hartboy, He'd shoot the Hell out of a leaf
if it moved. They call it Love, The coupling
goes on here. As for me, I'm a Toss and Turn
without my mynah bird, my fatigable, my bug.
Swung the sickle of the Flesh, I did;
Heard the thump of a body slumped to the ground.
I was sheer balls by the third hour of star-dark.
But Sonntag takes the prize, he has no Core.
He drags his walrus carcass to a party,
Plunks it down in the middle of the room,
Clicks his tongue as if chambering a shell,
and sweats like tall grass lush with rain.

How Live, How Love?

1.

A beast of some sort under her willowy legs
not the thrilling downslitherer from the tree
As when a black cloud shews its lightning to deep,
the suddfen erection of the prouf head. Gone
the snake's enchanting leather converse.
She trembles she is not ready to open her eyes just yet
it is all flight inside, Entrails stepping on each other.
Yes, how one's heart beat at his silky slip-down
and vista of red cloud masterly rude.
Now only this clatter of horses' hooves *graves*
running out into the fields. She feels like the flipped leaves
of the book men will call *the good book* (so the serpent sneered).
"I have such a dreadful premonition" She cries.
"Stay with me, bite my nipple, tell me this Isn't happening.
You at least are here beside me? Can you hear me
in this is it breathing I hear the death of?
Is the huge shell against my ear what he called the *sea?*"

2.

Some people stand before a Waterfall because it Wipes out the
rocks, Others simply want to hear it Sing. I am he, I am those. I
flame out in the Fog on America's shore. The feminine principle
with regular life and chair and blue apostrohes turns their heads

after kissing a machinist like me, A voice-bearer toiling in the
Dow of murk. A dove *whose "wing hardly bear"* limps Stupefied in
petroleum light, Light without mane or one foot walking on the
waters. How the world whimpers its famous late age. But always
the motor in a man's clock has been good only for a hundred miles,
the animal clock on its back Observed in passing by a woman
whose belly is plural humanity. Does she find his size comparable
to hers? Next question. He's the stalk of grain she harvests the heads
of, lets in, they live together in the oder of dead corn. May her eyes
the Huge eyes of the grass look up to when she cubes in slowly
tears, before all this dies.

3.

    How long I recognized the authentic voice, my blood subtle with
disease. I found myself on a coast where gulls thought they were
spray or darkness, they hurled themselves against the cliffs. Next
I Sheltered in a cardboard box from which a rubber doll's hand
Protruded, You would not have been so foolish as to take it. My ideas
were of a certain unfinished odor, Flour white, not so ugly as Yeast,
Pinking at sunset, like a scald. I never wanted was never Curious no
Melancholy vandal of the *I* was I. When tragedies opened their doors
to me, I hung back because of the Smell of Birth. I was a thing no
one had need of, I was happy then, there was nothing to hope for.
But one day I succumbed: I began to collect Goldfish. I thought
it would be Amusing to watch them wander around Hungry and
unable to Hold Still or Drown, Occasionally lipping some mite-sized
flake. The first one was a swishy-assed root, Then came a Clueless
dance of Yellow Caesuras, then a Large-eyed Virginia Woolf sort of
spook moving her mouth without speaking. I bore it well until I

brought home a Beauty I called Venus in a Plastic see-through bag as Bulbous as a woman's breast, Also a Booklet entitled "How to Keep Your Gold Fish Alive for Fifteen Days." She rolled over dead rather than swim the finite circle of the bowl. I gave up collecting living things, Withdrew my rubber arm from the world, No longer attempted anything gold and changeable having to do with life, *a system of hesitations and horrors.* For everything is possible except. I reside again in what is Not obliged to be false. I have made the disregarded my home, With all its poor . . .

The Breathing Place

This is the Dutch door with six glass saucer windows on the upper
    panel
This is the international orange Dutch door in the house by the sea
This the spectacle of waves bashing the rocks below the house
This the velocity of the spray tons of vaporized lilies
And this is the third bell of the Dutch ship in the 23rd psalm of the
    sea
Correction: this is the HMS Indomitable and this is Billy Budd
    sweetest of sailors on the wide sloppy water
Oh Billy fragile Billy you must be wary my friend for even in a
    crow's nest gazing at the copper sunset over the lachrymose sea
    you are still among men
These are the copper pans I shine each day in the chalk white house
    by the sea
I await you whoever you are on this chair made of minerals cooked
    in the hottest suns before galaxies formed to flash *goodbye we die*
    in every direction
This is my welcome my friend trusting you to mean me no harm
    for no one prepares a table before me and sets out the clear glass
    dishes for the wine
Can you see the rain pissing on the widow panes?
Outside is the furious blunder of creation some call hell
Here there is nothing to fear sit still be comforted all will be well
    for thou art with me

My friends if I have any friends may tell you I'm snappish

I have done yoga I now breathe easy

    among most quanta of the animal kind

Yes, even among folk who walk around with a sly coyote air and

    tricks to entrap their prey

Well I understand them their particles too have been cooked into

    meanness

But you are a dear one feeling quite at home in my creaking house

    by the blowing sea

Sit by this table of skyblue glass molecules a lovely crystallization

    from universal madness

Scientists theorize that the center of the Milky Way smells of rum

    and raspberry they want you to feel at home that's so sweet

I really can't have all this fidgeting when I'm talking to you

I have never been so happy to be with anyone as I am with you in

    this well defended house by the sea

You are as beckoning to me as the windows set like the six eyes of

    the sand spider in my orange door

Thank you for being with me as was permitted when the world

    was first sucked through the straw of forms and made to claw

    and fornicate and sail by the standoffish stars and hang a boy

    for being charming guileless and pretty

So it is that billions of folk can just sit and talk as you and I do here

    where uninvited the world has come

Bluely Boundless Sea

Jane dons a poplin bonnet and crosses the meadow and nimble
over the stile with no intention to avoid the difficulty skips on
to the village. She enters a drapery shop and closes out a bolt of
Regency Silk dirt-cheap at 4/3. *All the small bidding comes to the
sea*, she surprises herself by thinking. She drops the change into her
sealskin purse.

Orange fills half the sky in fiery diffusion. Could she have
forgotten to take the kettle off the stove? With steps as wild as script
where the letters are men's shadows tracked by a sea leopard under
a floe, she hastens homeward, her tears melting cows and trees.
Think, think clearly: had she been in the kitchen, preparing tea?
Or was she at the secretary thinking of having Lizzie put the kettle
on, before deciding it does not belong in literature, it is a thing the
servants do.

Now the sky is navy-colored cloud debris, the day showing its
bruises, which always appear a bit late following a horrid pinch.
Jumps. She jumps at the thought of the wind rising before she
can approach her smoking door. The stormy part of the story is
because there was no portrait of it already on the wall. Cowbells
clang toward her slangily off key, as when at a wedding a squall
sweeps in from the Atlantic and blows the floral arrangements to
bits and pieces. Yet generations survive gusts and burning houses

and walks to town and weddings. They take tea on the lawn in the summer, between showers. People talking quietly, in short ripples of conversation, like flutists and oboists warming up their instruments before the concert begins, then walking southward with strangers as far as animal behavior.

Listen: a seal's disgusting pump-honks where there should be no seals. She will be vexed indeed if she does not reach the house before dark. She would no longer recognize her life: she might as well be on a deck at dusk from which sailors had failed to throw back some fabulous wet creature so that she could walk about untrammeled. If the approaching ice floes begins to spell AUTHORESS, she will have to run even faster to get home.

Beethoven's Metronome

Mary Haycock   had a   fear of exposure (C sharp major);
as to that   even animals   copy.

If the original dies   what then? (C minor):
in the cellar   With the prisoners   refusal to eat.

I have known   Pilots crawl from
flaming cockpits   in the ceiling

and muddy Water   in rolling-leaf pattern
on the walls.

Who blackened the Map of the labyrinth?
Who pulled the Wings off the myths?

Peter Sloterdijk writes: "'Uprooting' is the meaning
of the modern   and takes on   a bright sound

and can be uttered   like a demand."
Oh, Peter! don't say anything so German   Unfeeling

or say it otherwise;   say "Walnut shells
floating on the water   as abandoned as Degas' heart

which the 'little rats'   stitched up   in a silk pouch
the faded pink of their pumps"   or "there's a Grove

in the psyche   where the leaves   never stir,
as regulated   as music paper   before the notes appear."

There Are the Old Grand Things Still

Pink and gray are the colors of evening I like most. Blood in the
Water. Orange. French. Gold.
Come to me in poetry, come inclined for society.
You are an example of water, Ample.
I am a certain distress in the landscape arising. my hands the sons
and daughters of the only food to be Grubbed out of the ground
and Picked from the trees and Shot through the head, torn up,
Brought down.
The main facts of life past and present if through the garden's fiery
tribes I stray.
The genitals are tracks in the woods.
The oak grows though the Barbara leaf. Oh come out from beyond
yon oak. We have to Deal with the chloride, our eyes through
the Ceiling Hard.
I am of northern blood. Repression binds the lingering night.
What comes near me departs.
Life moves like ice torn from a river.
Minerva is not a hexameter. Poets and the poor daily become more
docile. We Quit the notion of all verses.

Retrieval

I had a chaos and it rushing like they do
and everything only sub largo the moment
you go down to the weedy gods.

(there was tenderness) (the mouth gentle
over the feathers) (as a hand holds its first snow)

Bus

My vehicle is another life fluttering like a bird in a bath but stinking of Monet's lily-pond. I conceive you a little differently my honey in the canal of flowers. Your spirit is at times an animal innocence, improbable, drawn in incredibly narcotic lines. I would never drive off a cliff in your mild overcast, cat whose claws have striped the seats during sex, rolling on the meat and metal floor, our buds opening, our unavoidables.

I hang you from the window of the bus like a canteen, a banner of eyelids. I breathe you, my motor oil. "It is what I do that teaches me how to think."

Pedestrians flee, yelling obscenities. Your strongbox locked, I bang it open: empty – a ruse. Exhaust Clouds spray from my despairing love. You are as terrible as a beautiful boy.

In the morning, I conjure honey and fire. I crochet with my toes honey and fire. But *you* I could find only in quick stabs at reality's core. My bus is a panther in the jungles of Guatemala, its eyes look for your shoulders – intense, naked – among the giant-leaved plants, even as you laugh from the seat behind me, a belching laugh that goes through England and blows south among warlike men who glow on America's shore. You lecture me on the transformability of poetic material. "The next sentence needs to drink from the darkness where the pronouns are already drunk.

Capture the future. Demand commentary from the futurum." You mock my appeals for examples. "*Immortal demons of futurity*" – speaking in your sleep.

I could stop at a rest area and not wait for you to come out of the john, think of that? With one tire-smoking breakaway I could shed crates of spices, your distracted smile. See how you fare without my hippie musk, my ambiguous virility. I will choose not to hear you when you cry *voice come back*. The horrid length of your light will not read my night. I am tired, angel, tired. My eyes suck the afterglow into my dark. Why devote the remaining portion of my vanishing senses to an act of boldness?

Your softness was a peculiar nun spirit in the Peruvian wilds (did I say that?), a starry host tucked under the coif, lining the wimple and bandeaux. Or wasn't that you? Metamorphosis is your meadow. Lost in an illusion of grass.

Why was so little said of the centauresses of old? Were they not the wise ones? Did we meet at the races? You no longer drop coins into my box. You travel, now, on your own four feet.

My bus has been converted into the stone of night. I have not been to Guatemala for a hundred years. I drove off a cliff with my knees and liver. Like a mountain lion from its uprooted-tree-root den, like rifles with a bounty for demons, your thighs ran off as swift as a California fire, foregoing a coup de grace. The shore I lit upon was endless Content. The sea came at me like an enormous tongue.

I live in Paris now, and drive a bus. The door opens and closes on the passengers with a *whuff*, like a leather wing. In the rain and under the lights at night the pavements run with honey. But I miss the life of allegory, I am forbidden all joy.

Ferns, Fingers, Gorges

Music, his pubic hair against my ear. All his warm nests.
Worn train wheels Stick squeal first on one side, then the other:
so he parted. I slap my thighs.
He cables from a ship bigger than province:
that's his news. My Buck whose antler
I gripped. I liked my cheek
against his baby. I put my tongue on Time,
I cry and crouch in her blindswarm,
my vaulting lady.

Ovid on the Lake

I have danced in the woods of lewd refrains, written with sap
running from my mouth, virgin blood from my hands; I suffered
in anything netted by the gut-spiller Eros. Yet my rifle roots were
never shot; I persisted, I stood outside, I continued to *see*. Imagine,
then, my relief when at last I came to this height, the Bright Points
of my shoulders accurate in space, my belt a trio of matched stars.
But, alas, even now I am not as headless as I look. Gazing down
as I do, for instance, on this Canadian lake, the lone Rower in an
orange jacket water-Striding through aspen reflections. Together we
glide through the fallen beauties. Yes, I too dig my oars into those
yellow garments, I too cause that watery flesh to tremble. What
compels a person to look at anything whatever, say Down her dress
as she puts on your socks / your hands burnt, / Boards barricading
the door? To gaze and gaze only fakes everlastingness into things,
a delusion on an earth that spins blue, green, white, night, blue.
Malicious gossip once had me attempting to rape my love, Artemis;
had her trying to kill me in return (actually, she was a dear one).
But I can't be guarded, it still ripples through me, the longing to use
sight like a spade; violently to worm in. And will you judge me, you
who all your life slice oars into the Wet membrane that supports
you? Can you not walk alone with your hands on your head down
the center of a rain-swept town? Withdraw now, withdraw your
mad attention to life.

Breathless

if breath were a sort of gigantic torso
with all possible earths in it, all Hatchling
molecules; If it could be jacked into the music
of Many Fountains starting up Together . . .
but its legs are hair-thin it can be
Stopped by a tune a cough a chile.
Poor breath it *will* fight for air like Persephone
fleeing barefoot in the underworld tar,
her summer frock ruined into beauty
in the eyes of her creepy husband.
It *must* leave behind the touted honey
and hundred whips of love
and all the best paintings in Paris,
held off in an exact little stone.

What Was to Be an Elegy for Emily Dickinson

Why should there be red shoes if the earth was never born,
it was never born and these are its red shoes,
these the cerise Atlantic clouds to be taken with no comedy
remainder, why should there be a suchness of the day,

when a lightning suspender is no union. Alas, the long
and beautiful person is in a cold house and the
slippery walks have no standing, the grass with its green
javelins, the cloud's red slaughter and the beautiful

person dead; I shall not enumerate when Uallach,
daughter of Muimhneachan and chief poet of Ireland,
died still thinking there were letters of the alphabet
too small to detect, and had no reaction

to the surface winds of difference,
no, no shaking of the head, no story when the story
is the evening and the laughter of drowned children
riding under water on the horses of the King

of the West.
When I met her, a year above now,
she showed me the sunshine
of the country and a cairn of red shoes.

Herds of Stags Among Fir Trees

"I can hardly hold my face together," I tell the moon,
"when I see you smile. Oh, to touch the sea's belly
with *my* belly amidst a crowd of jellies.
To loom brassy behind a scrim of rain.

"But lately you seem aloof," I add, "as if you regard
the ripples of things, not the things themselves.
When the trees email the birds to come in the spring
and the sun thanks them with cyan atoms for their song,

"Is it anything to you? Not that You should care
that the Hobermans release their Dobermans
on their vast estates. If one should ask how to get
to the Capitol, you would point Indifferently and say,

"'there, on the earth.' After all, you're nothing of us
except some DNA of the same dust. When the last breath
is Feared, then Known, and we throw ourselves on the
beloved body because a flood of purple blood

"suddenly belittles that dear face, What comfort
could you give? We won't care then about a gaudy light
in the sky or succumb to that perfect lie:
'the murder at the roots is in love with the trees'?"

Self-Portrait as Absence of Days

In Memory of 'Annah Sobelman

The particles of this night have been recalled.
The Spectrum is black that has no electric substance.

        The ménage of this night
is you the Pale horse the reader in the zone
of bachelors whose bride lacks evidence of temporal life.

She lies in Cold clouds of sheets somewhere in the Lumpy dark:
        She Cannot hear the bright icy notes
of the small white stars
        or Oboes warm in the Red ones.

She will come down as the brief morning rain.

                    *   *   *

        Why I am shaking is because I have never Shook
this salt on the river before,
shaken this Rain, the silver salt of this Rain –
though all sorrow is different and the same.

My bright Rainloves startle up from the river
in a frantic goodbye; They are already river,
They have falldn onto its horizontal with a shock,

you see they could not know they'd be Stopped cold
so very low. I weep for those who die Shivering so,
Shaming my good luck.

* * *

She is beyond the need of embraces now,
beyond Rossini, who coupled with her in a dream
that made her cry from so much Music
in the music,

it had been so long . . .

* * *

When I die, I will be a fire-ring of stones
the color of a shabby Mattress
where hobos fuck each other or Runaway girls and boys
who stop at the Smell of Cooking , , .

Who says I don't get to choose?

* * *

At first you feel excited by your Abilities,
As Elvis was, okay?
Then already the scarlet Blush of closure
deepens to the Slap bass of the sea,
Stormics take hard against you, Drowning

your wasp nest fragiles   ·
saved from the groans and ash of the burning woods.

*   *   *

Comes the moment when, Flashlight dead,
You cannot go farther into the abandoned mine,
You cannot return:

There was no cry of "fire in the hole."
But there is always fire in the Hole.

Winds from the Wilderness

1

That the feeling has a meaning,
Sweetwater dancing persisting,
Makes an eddy, snaring.
But the song of the Stream
Cannot thunder. We will find out,
We promise,
How to sing off-key
Like thunder.

2

Now we speak such and such
In cooled-down Digital mouth.
Have read all about it,
        the new age,
It sounds swell.
To circumnavigate
        the eddies
On black and white faint-thudding
Plastic feet,
Raindrops on a skylight –
It sounds swell.

What's that?" the digitalarians ask.
"Sounds like singing."

3
Singers intervene
When a thousand eddies
Feed like maggots
On their mother
And maple trees
Fry yellow in the frost.

4
Are the singers
Off key or do they seek roots
In the western Thrush,
Teeth in the Tamarack?
You can't ride on the back
Of a mite on the back
of an owl.

They dream late from the confessionals
Of a hollow tree.

5
That the sexual life
Of an eddy is Anonymous,
Not signed Eliot, George,
Or T. S., her frightened footman;

That it sucks down
The dreams they bought,
Is the cruelty I speak of in section five.

What is a song without excess?
Destructive to humanity.
What molests the song?
Unshakeable ancestry.

6

Lift the eyelid of the Age –
(The Mandelstam test):
Yellow. Thought so:
The age is Critical.

Ages with a Critical Function
Make no difference in the stream:
No age makes a
difference in the stream.
Eddies, and still more eddies,
Replace, and replace
The dream.

7

I dreamt I washed history's feet
With the downpour of my tears.
It was in a play.
Catullus was there, cat calling:
"Ticket of milk!"

I took that to mean
There was not enough cat in the dream.

8
Dream not and The end will come early,
If there is an end, and we promise.
To survive the end of the dream
Is the beginning.

And now we take on Everything . . .
song with Rogue shadows
and the Splendor of white galaxies.
We are afraid.

2.

The Era

Obscenity the First Language of Soldiers

Go on, Nation State, bunch your Clouds up
like a Wall at Nightfall, while the sun, even so,
burns umbilical cords & blood astonishing.
What you fear is the mauve lining of Capitol
clouding in evening's most threatening hour;
that it may catch fire, Rain down fire.
Yes, be wary of the people in whose living
you sit, flattering their DNA of greatness.
Somewhere the person in them, in their socks,
in their shoes, knows or certainly will know
how heavily you stand on the Eagle's neck.

The cosmic winds' shifting tents do better
at Housing the least of things, if flappingly –
why, almost intimately under black and violet
clouds. Even the helpless are clasped
by the Bell-Curves' gravity, built tough
if not enough to withstand the Hammer,
the Fate of the images. We are not weeping
here. The river is sharp, *the knife is shining
the sweetness,* but not Your knife, Master
of jealous funds, Slasher.

I, Dionysus, went to the House of the Mad
to free my mother. We swam across Lake Alcyonius
as if through liquid metal. Her nightgown
was a great white fish, very heavy to drag
to the other side. She was, after all, only mortal,
by name Semele, so Death was already
deep inside her, but no more about that.
Her Care-taker uncle gave her syphilis,
but no more about that. From poverty
comes a smell of arms and legs lying around,
but you wouldn't know about that.

I think of the black children holding up the sign:
WE LOVES YOU, BOBBY to the passing train,
and more often of the toddler
Kennedy knelt before on a delta shack's floor,
weeping because he could not call it back,
it did not know its name.

When communism fell athwart the human
psyche's power winds, some few
of the surviving spirit's dying headlights
lined the shore but failed to reach
the muddy waters of neglect. Entered days
of strange behavior. Gall rose in the milk
glass of the spine, Apollo wailed like a gull
wind-whipped around the sky. Poetry's resistance
slackened, gray, with some rain.
I found myself amid the people of the

Sundial, who stood still,
while their shadows crept in circles.

Is this the way forward now, the horror
of bald ego gloom? The windshield
of compassion, bucking the Abyss, shattered?
How long we had failed to understand
that the wilderness was ours, is us,
that Fair is only an experiment.
Unaware, the House continues to sit.

The Era

The white crisis, the white House
blood type, White essences,
millions of White Accidents,
those on the way it goes
White from here, white Lighthouse
stinging the sea, All angels
marvelous unsavory whose white cysts
Swell in the shadows of white placentas,
pages of white moths, and How now
achieve, in all the white accommodation
(the white tiger drinking from the star stream),
the definitive shredding of white subpoenas
(not a whitewash, no, not a whiteout, no),
as one snatches away a white Veil –
suddenly she Had to leave, Stopped short
in the midst of white Arches,
had to run away, stopped Cold
by a Crowd of white hellos,
they swoop so dizzyingly,
How long can this go on,
but had we been so very kind
so very clever as to sift the white sugar
glass from the rain, taken the hands
of the Ruler Gods, strolled

like freshets of air into this hour,
smelled the green, the astonishing change,
cleared the log jams of scrolled-up
white wedding dresses, mothballed
they are, tied with cold memories,
climbed the white cliffs in our millions of moths,
could we have Helped her,
How long can this go on,

Could she be deeply affected again,
Freed by Tall Claps of impermanence,
sprigged with whoozit atoms,
our only money,
the Rulers folding Paper airplanes
out of their countless white Documents,
old white causes, type: white angelism –
but See where she Halts beNumbed
in the white halls of stay as you are,
dressed white on white in the crisis of surveillance,
who can stop this, the whole white colony
Amassing shares, drones ready to bomb
infestations Crossing lawns with Suitcases?

No Leaf Will Shade

No use to us, he will Not fish us out, he doesn't have a Pole
to fish us out, the Dark husband the too much husband.

I take the Last Spoon from the Dead Father's mouth.

Fleeing from his famous need to be cruel,
Pollock painted equivalence, unscalable, indivisible,
eliminating roads, and

el mas terrible de todos los sentimentos.

Maybe you like it here, in Twentieth-something,
unraveling? All my asks are lost in the infra-red,
unable to farm, water, dawn . . .

From the wound of being male,
even the jaded will stare at her stage-lit breasts
those soothing somethings. But big boys
fear the Bulging mother of the race, the flood
from which they have never dried out.
They retreat to manipulable funds.
The garden is a gulf in the intercom.

Once when he called on me, the husband,
I promised to send my wife to him – his wife, that is –
in a work of outdated marble. Wives are history's women
before they are "my woman," foregone.

I walk in the halls of Abstract Painting one leg off and one leg on.

Sat Down and Wept By Lake and Cloud Gear

1
Two police cars outside: flush yr Centaur.

The sea-squids of the congresses
swim among the flooded people;
a star urinates over Cupcake mountain;
cloud livers drip on the gardens.

We take it as a sign, pixelated –
we, a short fever in space
combining
ones and the empty sign for nothing.

2
Love tall clouds, how they mistake
a Dupont pond for a lake
on which to launch paradisal
meadows of white clover.

How much money is needed
to keep the poor agreeing to be poor?

O bathtubs in Flint, no one lingers in you now,
Playing with his willy.

3
Tell us, POTUS, does the U. S.
S. Missouri tickle your palm, the guns a-cock?
Your subs hop up and down
like the fleas in the blocks in Auschwitz,
"thousands of little fountains on the floor,"

4
Remember Song?
She loved it that we wooed her.
Who?
      The used,

            the Green genius of the mute.

                 was she not the one for you?

5
The nymph is out of her grotto:
disgrace of a Nation,
worked oilily from behind,

          the dirtiest things.........

The tires are burning pianos!

Cuba in 1959, a bit of Reality happened.

After which:

Vietnam,

Afghanistan,

Iraq,

Yemen,

Syria,

Birds of Washington

"I want people who love us. I don't want people coming in the way they do now." Not the Veery people, who migrate at night for safety and keep together by a contact call. Nor the Widgeon people, who sleep on tiny rafts far out from shore.

Bushtit miles of pendulous breast-nests on Pennsylvania Avenue. Permanent juvenile's Supreme court nominee, a permanent juvenile, approved.

The Solitary Sandpiper lays its eggs in Songbirds' nests, crowding out the children of the Robin, Rusty Blackbird, and Gray Jay. It doesn't have any friends; it doesn't want any friends. Alert: Mexican eggs, Honduran eggs, all brown eggs, watch your backs.

The Common Loon is sneaky, it creeps along beside boats, it dives and steals fish from the line. What a Loner's Cackle! Its audience the Echoing lake. Ecstatic self-reviews. "The greatest speech ever."

I am the woman seen reading *Citizen* behind the President's speech. Of course I am not a Real person, I am a Paid activist. I advocate open borders and migrations in sky-blackening flocks. I eat rodents grasshoppers and flies. My diseases are legion, I give birth in abandoned buildings, I give birth on the ground.

"Terrible! Just found out that Obama had my 'wires tapped.' Mc-Carthyism!"

"I won't ever make you read more than a page on any decision, Mr. President."

"Terrible! Terrible!"

Tweeting in the vehement easter of early mornings.

I Am a Circle until I Become a Power

From the Button in my heart let's Bomb something.
We are Destiny's baron is what they tell me
in the little room in the Robin's absence.
Rum is everything, lining up to buy gasoline
for the Last hundred miles from the Logos.
The landscape shimmers in Methane,
good for a thousand years. These Country airs
are fluted flatulence. Neighboring counties
"none can see, the earth and the air are
full of feathers, and these shut out the view,"
as Herodotus reported.
All a button wants to do is Bloom.
PRESS, then; it will be INCREDIBLE.
You will NOT BELIEVE.
Priceless stones are hiding in the marigolds.

Supervising the Woods

There must be no crawlies, runnies, eaters here.
Full of Chest, my nose can detect them.
   I spread my primeval wings for the Flyover.
    There! an encampment of fugitives.
I can't bear to tell you what happened next . . .

All around, Abominations. Beetles with
   Christ child, abdomens that Gurgle
    disgusting confessions.
No one has the belief I have: I show you
God splattered at the West end of my thumb.
   And I a mere poet with kill codes locked up in charms.

      All attempts on my muse
are met with . . . cough . . . wait: something in the ferns
Giving "free reign to its passion" (if that's
   the disgusting expression).
I took care of it; I use the plainest methods.
I was born for Love, probably, but the world's
   spores came at me like meadows of flame.

Have you ever fallen backwards
                   in your chair? Just so
the world falls away from me in my moments of weakness,

though the smell lingers on, the after-image of woods
with surgical breath, red Devil Claw berries, the piss-
   smell of ancient memory, throatless soughing:
   Can there be enough of that Essence-of-nothing
   Moaning behind you? Yes, enough. Get hunting.
Get hunting again.

                    It was originally war
brought on this cold Fever, the guards
   rubbing their breasts in my face,
   Lace underwear scattered in the undergrowth,
white crosses burning in the cradles,
Emerald-colored whistles of birds
fired from the windows of the Armory.

I am Occurrence in the midst of Appearances,
   and like Vallejo, will die of life, not time.
Roll around in your Wounds, you others, if you must,
but I sit on Top of the picture, seldom looking down,
            my legs dangling above Famines in the grass,
oil fields, the sub-Sahara, Car bombs, everything as dirty as I am.

                    Each afternoon, a miniature
White House bleats on my porch.
I hear the locks Disengage:
a tiny president comes out to address the nation.

Thin Bible-Paper Skies

Landscape regretted its remoteness at 4:40 p.m.,
    November 21, 2044.
        The Moment was recorded in Amber ink.
    The earth had not Coded itself yet, remember;
        it was still peeled to the Crotch.
The crisis seemed small but it proved a portent.

Now, though shapes remain, are they Real?
        Or Reversed in trembling water,
        a glug-glug mob, the Ashes of Sola?

"How'n you find me here, who is gilly pop, who is gully sack?"
    asked the creature we came upon on the road.
    The last entry in *Bartlett's* was
        "77 darknesses move. As was foretold."

Dinners of forbidden herbs for converting Rot into protein,
    Our hair gone, as if in punishment for Smelling of the enemies'
hair
        candied in Flame
            while we slept through cries coming from somewhere
remote:
        seals singing to the vanished herring,
        boat people calling for help from the water.

Our good American ears deep in sleep under Star-spangle.

　　　．

The grass stains on our knees won't wash out they
　　　　Show we were not The Chosen.
We are the Heavens Came Down the Mountains Poured Down
　　　　like Boiling Water
till Hatred Raised Them Up Again.
　Naturally, then, for thousands of years
　　Sensitive souls (that pathetic lot)
　　　　have longed to be *atmosphere vaporeuse.*

One day you came to me like a Dizzy Mountain
　Sweet Mountain falling into dust and love.
How could I help but see you as my RACK&STUFF,
　Love having been already tagged in Rome.
Barely encamped, we are Clubfooted in Star Time.

3.

Green Water

Los Vientos de Mi Vida

Limits everywhere. E.g., the Rose
　　　　has too many wings to Fly.
And the Stomach, how it digs
a tunnel to a bitter end.
Tell me what you feel, the torn fabric of the flame.
What you feel is what you are, is my thesis.
There *could* be something more, but what
good is it if it's sleeping Deep down,
Its sock Toes standing up like white Peaks
with mountain Goats, never exciting you
 except when you want to make love
Like a normal animal person?
I myself have the circumference of a circumflex,
But Memory proves that I'm in Motion.
The chickadee, the water-lily – are They in the same motion?
My calves are restless before a storm I feel myself
working into. Water is my Soldier, the torrent
taking off its gloves and pouring like Iodine
down a mile of incline. My Cayuga
flowers into the wild. I am so full of the Day
is a glorious feeling, like the French colon,
open on Each Side. I am chalk on a blackboard,
Dusty. I write wind, I write Palestine.

Absalom in the Flower's Throat

Any good wood is my Warm forest tongue,
In the air trembles the Ulysses of the leaves.
Mine is the green envelope zipped Open to the Groin,
Mine the gentle giant in his Orange sweater.
He hasn't galloped off with anyone, do you see?
He stands here & Flattens my foot, my loot.
Sometimes he Cradles me who is strangely quiet.
No evil attracts him, not if you let him
Saddle your day, Fish in your stream.
He smiles with his horns.
Where he was born
The cedars, incondite, are as shaggy as sherpas.
Look into his eyes: It that your father you see,
Shining an apple on his hip? Do you know that tongue,
like a fish? And hers, dark hair swept over it?

Solo Rip

Here, no one comes to breed me
open, wanting me close,
as when the dentist says,
"Open wide." I
Circulate like Shears
In the ungoverned tissue
of my world. *They,*
on the other hand, the Worthy
couple within me,
never finish crying or hoping;
they don't like
the wounds I've taught to Thunder.
They'd stand on my Shoulders
and Soar if they could
but are still on all fours in their genome.
To win me over they remove
their clothes and display their
Complementary Parts,
but then– quick! – cover them over
with pink knitted things for baby.
They dream of Recasting the soul
as a temple of middle-classness,
but I know they'd settle for
an afternoon far from my pile

of Throwing stones, from which
they borrow when they quarrel,
and a neck that's Not the fourth
bone of the pelvis.

As they gaze at the Vast Toccata
of the icy night sky,
how grateful they are
for the touch of a warm hand on their ass,
one ounce of pressure
per square inch.
Will there ever be any two
in the world Not cornered
in this same dimension?
So One is larger than Two,
is my thesis, the terrible openness of one.
You get to lick everything around you.
You whistle and the weird birds come.

Seven of my Sweet Loves Drove off of Cliffs

Seven more dragged a baby blanket steaming like a horse.
As for me, I hid in a train as lengthy as the earth-line,
an outlaw stinking louder than the cattle-whiff straw.
How face the specters of the twelve regrets?
Somewhere a deer was being torn apart.
Of course I was fuck in the loft when lightning stunned the barn;
I myself was the Dry-rot wood, I was the Crackle.

*   *   *

Tonight, in an ecstasy of disease, hair
dangles from blackening clouds.
but at eighty-three I am past caring.
My brother is Bravado, my sister, Bluster.
I have a few winds left to slice through to the sea.
Feathered in the corrupt finance of destiny,
I close my eyes and flap like the empty sleeves of the air.

Like a Waterfall Seen from the Lip, More Felt than Seen

You all tell me about the power of Ideas,
but what if thinking in the dirt need be done,
what then? You need to fly too low for guns to shoot,
baby the carrots, the Sunset-Orange roots.

Yes, brush the vultures from the flesh-shack roof.
but know that *particular disorders are a kind of Beauty*
in the universe – or so Malebranche said (and I agree
if he means

but it's too late to ask him what he Means).
Say an idea sliced in two with a hoe
is a grow and you jump in
(you could be a disorder in the universe) –

then the thrill, for instance, of WHITE SHADOWS
coming up CHILL from the FALLS, tho it STILL be FEAR –
the World-stomach dissolving your frame
could STILL BE FEAR.*

* Would you know this pleasure if it were not for the traces of fear, the sensation
  of the roiling of terrible liquids in your organs when you were born on Perseus,
  whose profound B flat, majestic and joyful, takes billions of years longer to form
  than the Ode to Joy?

What Breathes mountains, the First air walking around
with No clothes on, for one minute, maybe two,
is not an idea.

Then a tiny blue backpack moving away . .

Singing in Octaves with the Breakfast Robins

Her eyes came back to the house
Singing in Octaves with the breakfast robins.
The door is open. She goes out again:
On the Walkway, a lizard the color of wild lettuce . . .
She will watch any little thing that is boiling.

Ah, but Evening! What to do
But turn it around and around,
Like a Ring on an Itching finger?
Eyes Done now with their meal of birds
("I had a Chaffinch today,"
   smacking their lids),
They Crawl over the darkening bay
Like a bee on a Sail, their chemical lamps
Hanging low over the turnip purple of the Sea.

Asleep, they Roll around under their Lids,
As if mad to break out to the Bling
Flashing over the harbor. O Credulous ones,
It's just dust and ignited gas:
The earth Alone is yours, a lover in full
Till night calls you into the shady grove.

The Persistence of the Particular:
a letter to the painter Brian Shields

Like all abstract expressionists, dear friend, you have forgotten
the names and shapes of things, but I know what your work is
hiding – that is, poetry knows. For instance, in the painting of
three stepped mountains (are they mountains?) rising up to the
day moon I can see, in the smallest one, so vividly it must be true,
bicycles making adjustments to fragrances, pine and rabbit, & a
narrow stream striped like a slice of raw bacon flowing à la the Rio
Grande in the charity of it last days. Also a diary dropped on the
road. Puffs of breath everywhere – yours, probably.

In the pug valley behind the hill, I see blue, blurry trees –
no, not trees – erupt into a sword fight – no, not swords! Why
are nouns so hasty, so premature? Oh, Brian, have I toyed with
something sacred? Are colors and fragmentary shapes truer to the
emotions, our immediate reality, than words? Didn't you once say,
"All these literati think they can play the art critic, as if painting
weren't the least accessible thing of all" – or was that Degas? . . .
Let's see, where was I? Space, disruption, stabbings, the need for
violence just there.

On the second mountain, famous for its blue yodeling, skiers
cut narrow silk wagon tracks into fresh powder. In the chalet below,
I read as if inside a walnut knocked on by sleigh & church bells.

Later, I snowshoe into evening in the pink atmosphere Ceres strikes from the necks of descending doves. Overhead, Venus chirps.

The third mountain is mammoth, it's top is coming off. The villagers think it was hit by the last century's bombings. Here lightning is the sex. The scent of assassins is strong.

At this elevation, space is empty & final. Your native Spain & adopted Taos would have it so. But that blue-green moon you say is not a moon is pulling and being pulled, squeezed like a water balloon or a wrestler's face smushed against a mat. Kinetics is your love, or one of them; the tension with gravity – the damn stuff being everywhere. Even so, Brian, you're heedless of borders, like all epic beings, while, even in a century of hard breathing, you're gentle & patient. You do not wish to see at any height Ceres slice the necks of doves to drink new life.

And I After So Many Words . . .

Purple Squiggles locked in black squares,
parroty flitters in the shadows:
      a studio mentality is suspected,
a Swim in substance without a duck or back,
     on the Wild side of nomadic narrative.

  Heigh ho, Joan Mitchell, heigh ho, Cy,
let us walk with you thru Bright Refigurings,
   Climb, rather, up your Color cliffs,
              like the tiny figures in *King Lear*
who Harvest Samphire, which smells of the day
when color first emptied its Buckets onto the world.

We begin dirty, don't we, loves, Hoisted out of the organs' Slick,
     and washed Shiny,
like a raddish;
but it's Greasy kisses you love and that I Love that you love:
   Not for you a mastiff and beat-up
   Red gas can in the back of a Pickup;
not for you empiricism's virile bench press,
    like US troops arriving in Iraq.

Squarely you face toward the Blast that got us here in a Perfect Offence
    to reason—
something unthinkably too tiny for scale but that could *hold it in no more,*
    all that Feeling, the rage to be extravagant –
the same provocation that made Hildegard babble of "purple lightning"
    and van Gogh poke the world's eye with a yellow stick.

So let's throw confetti and more confetti
Upon the color vanguard. Praise to their palettes
that challenge the transparency of tears.

Blessed Disorder

Napoli. Drove into considerable laundry
Spotting the grubby darkness.
No, no; no watch.

Boat to Capri
throbbing like a washing machine.
The heart Mimics the Moist haze.

An Italian scratches his crack at the rail,
as three French people break into "The Isle of Capri."

Roma. Maybe you like? You pay me?
Water laughs in the Trevi.
The babies Laugh. The birds Laugh.

Running, one Gets Through the Vatican, breathless,
laying the meaty nudes to Rest.
Stupid omission of birds, hard-ons, a bit of fun.

Out on the Country Roads
motorcycles pass in their oily undershirts.
Poppies spank the green.
Another woman goatherd,

another *Crucifixione*,
Amen, Amen.

Firenze. Leonardo's feathered armpits.

Assisi. White oxen glowing in late afternoon light,
the last living fresco.

I know you, impersonality,
drinking like the lily the living waters.

Sunny Flow from Little Barks

Author of yes, *conversant* sun, today's word from Delphi
    is *delphinium*: expensive
blue word, dust payment due tomorrow.

Over the Ponte Vecchio, past the cantaloupe-orange shops
    glittering with proxies of your gold, A girl
of cappuccino color walks in your transparent hem.

She rubs a pineapple cube along my lips,
    the coffee girl, a dram of sun, sourced from the Source,
sorcerer of earth and dread Venus and ruddy Mars.

A moment *petulante* presses her jasmine upon the air, cream, velvet,
    then this thing happens with this guy, this green young gray guy,
    and I feel
there are "dimensions" that get "uncornered" in the fun.

We go rummaging in the shops, the girl the guy the sun and I,
    softening white chocolate Davids in our mouths—
the heads and overlong arms and legs brittle to begin with, then
    goo.

One street and one street over, There's not a single David left,
only a strange plenitude an Organic resolve like potatoes growing
    baby potatoes from their eyes.

For fragrant encryptions, go inside the Boboli doughty dada tangle
    of greens.

A cool moment now in Fiesole as I place under a clear bowl of
    grapes this little cloud.

I Want to Walk with You in the Roaring Gardens

The windows lavish their affection on the robins,
they Rake the yard for them, Slight the elms.
The garden is Humid. The heroines of Unhappy love
release a scream in the form of a Fountain.

Today it snows. Flake by Flake,
a white Beatrice gathers herself in my arms,
her Image with lowered eyes
an allusion to the Veiled governance of matter.

Away paddles the white Swan of day
in an Entourage of ripples. White swan,
Black swan, share the planetary waters.
            As if to share were a Universal given.

To share is a universal given.

Electromagnetic waves
pour through the darkened house,
Grasshopper-quick troubadours,
flashing ruby, chartreuse, the Circle of the hills.

First light Stirs from the abyss.
A Cloud lets fall a Sob of grain.

Vermin spin in the garden. Gadarene
the hyacinths' Involuntary Beauty.

Health, the trident, Pokes at the blubbery sea.
A thousand years flash in Each Freed Sparkle.
Does anything reconcile destiny? Only,
perhaps, the Eurydice of the Moment

just before Orpheus doubts her. She, too,
Springs from brilliant gas, Vast lianas of dust,
the Mathematical Order of the elements;

and where else but from there come the Orange breasts,
the fountain's quarreling Mouthfuls,
the Elms shouldering their Leaves?

Canoeing a Worn River

I

    Alphabet of tiny paddles, is no bird sewn onto you? Is there
no seating for animal leaves in your auditorium?
You, laid out as for row composition, but a solvent scrambler,
cued by other transitives.

The wind imprints on the water its fingertip whorls, or is it
    "Hello"?

Your paddles would be hands-on too, nimbly altering water's
    complexion.
But, really, you yourself are the swell and ripple;
for, as Hegel said, you are the "in," the paddle

        Spank and Traction.

Yes, one pull forward and you're published separately.
Two, and your motifs spread romantically.
Wet slick slip of the pen starts the flow.

You cannot be the water? We are tired of hearing this.
For neither can the water be water, wet and slick, unless you name
    it so.

You like it that way—arrogant forwarder that you are.
Namer. Changer. Arranger.

You mutter something about cosmic splutter, matter's splatter,
"the twisted glass shirt of the river." An image you like,
You take it from Peter Redgrove, thief that you are.

Red grove, red grove, red grove. It's yours now. You have no shame.

2

River's dissolve-speech. Listen to the driveling discussion.
Inarticulation is the assassin. It shifts its feet,

a destroyer of patterned reruns.
Its ripples retract themselves like snake tongues.

      Drifting

footprints, loosed from their garrison . . .

Alphabet-kit, you can't support Jesus Bugs,
but you are ultra-employable.

Con man on the bank has games for you,
stunning properties, funiculars to the infinite.
Ignore him, you can have so much more,
 a departure from

Night

is not here for you. You go

Directly,

go riddle, go charm.

From the standpoint of semiotics,
we propose the

Aping

of currents in the currents, the chafing of limits
in the fashion of water's pulsing pliancy.

Someone should second the motions of the real,
mimic the cat's paw, the rock obstacle.
Say "Hello," say "I announce," say, "the

Empirical

river, the outer world, is just what is not in the world."

Hegel discovered the trick of it: Appearance is
strictly restricted, it mists over, it

Reappears

intact. It can't be more mineral vegetable or cat
than it is. It's *your* word and world, dear alphabet,
that appears to change it

Existentially,

changes even as *it* changes. Paddle

Forward
and you're published separately, like

Sunset

on the water.

Reflections

play with the rules. You were borne paddling,
your motifs romantically distributed.

Secondary Appearances, challenging the Primary ones,
are now holding their

Exhibition

at the Durand-Ruel gallery,
with greenish deliquescence by M. P. Marcel-Béronneau
and gold fish all over Paris.

Do the Two levels of Appearance.
sensory and written, agree?
Not strictly in your lifetime.

Do they make a Third? Not likely.
The world is still short a

Sum

when you are on the river, riverrun.

3

A dissolve speech; look at the driveling.
The speaking being is not the assassin,

Billboards on the banks, prospects
for mines on Mars and the moon.
But, again, You can reach even farther,
to headless

Night's

black buttercups
blowing in quantum fields,
if only you speak them.

Your canoe

Shakes

upon the waters. Paddle, little conveyances
of the ever-more-enormous material world,
work with and against its slipperiness;

Engage;

Lower your oars for the recommencing.
Tease, deny, the restrictions only art can alter.

Do the two then make a third? Do they?

Where? Unknown auditorium.

NOTES

Now and again, this collection echoes (adopts, adapts) material from William Blake, César Vallejo, Tomaz Salamun, and Federicke Mayröcker. The epigraph from Mayröcker's poem "Narrating of a Narration" is in Rosemary Waldrop and Harriet Watts' translation in *The Vienna Group: Six Major Austrian Poets*, p. 39.

The principal sources of "Birds of Washington" are *Fear* by Bob Woodward, *Birds of Washington: Field Guide*, and *National Audubon Society Field Guide to North American Birds: Western Region.*

The title "Bluely Boundless Sea" comes from Melville's *The Encantadas;* that of "Winds from the Wilderness" from John Donne's sermons. The poem "There Are Grand Old Things Still" collides at points with phrases and quoted lines of verse in John Ruskin's *Selected Writings* (Oxford World's Classic). The titles "Singing in Octaves with the Breakfast Robins" and "Herds of Stags among Fir Trees" (the latter slightly altered) are lifted from Gerard Manley Hopkins' notebooks. Blanca Varela's "my belly touches the sea's belly," as translated by Kristen Dykstra, is adapted in the latter poem.

Both of the passages pertaining to Degas derive from Roberto Calasso's *La Folie Baudelaire*, translated by Alastair McEwen. "Bus" quotes the painter Pierre Soulages's statement, "It is what I do that teaches me what to think," and adapts Osip Mandelstam's statement that Dante's cantos "demand commentary in the *futurum*" and echoes his expression "the transformability of poetic matter." My thanks to Sawnie Morris for suggesting the title "Los Vientos de Mi Vida," which played into the development of the poem. The title "Canoeing a Worn River" is drawn from Barbara Guest's poem "Borderlands."

I omit, for want of exact memory and fear of exhausting the reader's patience, the numerous imprints from many other sources, especially the many poets whom I have found deliciously absorbing.

ACKNOWLEDGEMENTS

Versions of some of these poems appeared in *Bennington Review*, *Boston Review*, *Denver Quarterly*, *Fence*, *Hunger Mountain*, *Iowa Review*, *Los Angeles Review of Books Quarterly Journal*, *Oversound*, *PEN Poetry Series*, *Poetry International*, *New American Writing*, and *Taos Journal of International Poetry and Art*. I am most grateful to the editors.

My heartfelt thanks to friends Forrest Gander, Kenneth Lincoln, Richard Greenfield, and Sawnie Morris, who helped me with earlier versions of some of the poems. Later, Forrest Gander and Brenda Hillman combed through what might have been the final manuscript if their acumen hadn't made it better. My dear friend 'Annah Sobelman, so sharply missed, continues to speak support into my ear. This book is dedicated to her memory.

Calvin Bedient was raised in Washington state and got his Ph.D. in English literature at the University of Washington, after studying piano at the Whitman College Conservatory of Music. His first teaching position was at Emory University in Atlanta, Georgia. He then taught at the University of California until his recent retirement. He has been a visiting instructor at Harvard University and the Iowa Writers' Workshop. A founding editor of the New California Poetry Series, he now co-edits *Lana Turner: A Journal of Poetry & Opinion*. His reviews have appeared in *The New York Times Book Review*, *The New Republic*, *The Nation*, *Partisan Review*, *Salmagundi*, *The Boston Review*, and still other magazines. His critical books include *Eight Contemporary Poets* (Oxford University Press), *He Do the Police in Different Voices: The Waste Land and its Protagonist* (University of Chicago Press), and *The Yeats Brothers and Modernism's Love of Motion* (University of Notre Dame Press). He has published three previous collections of poetry: *Candy Necklace* (Wesleyan University Press), *The Violence of the Morning* (University of Georgia Press), *Days of Unwilling* (Saturnalia Books), and *The Multiple* (Omnidawn). He lives in Santa Monica, California.

The Breathing Place
Cal Bedient

Cover image by Brian Shields, *Piano,* 2018.
Oil, Gesso, and Graphite on Canvas. 59 x 67 inches. www.brianshieldsart.com
Courtesy of Brian Shields and Michael Warren Contemporaty Gallery,
Denver, Colorado.

Cover typefaces: Couturier and Frutiger
Interior typefaces: Frutiger and Adobe Garamond

Cover and interior design by adam b. bohannon

Printed in the United States
by Bookmobile, Minneapolis, Minnesota
On Rolland Enviro Book 70# 392 ppi Natural 100% PCW
Acid Free Archival Quality Recycled Paper

Publication of this book was made possible in part by gifts from
Katherine & John Gravendyk in honor of Hillary Gravendyk,
Francesca Bell, Mary Mackey, and The New Place Fund

Omnidawn Publishing
Oakland, California
Staff and Volunteers, Fall 2020

Rusty Morrison & Ken Keegan, senior editors & co-publishers
Kayla Ellenbecker, production editor & poetry editor
Gillian Olivia Blythe Hamel, senior editor & book designer
Trisha Peck, senior editor & book designer
Rob Hendricks, *Omniverse* editor, marketing editor & post-pub editor
Cassandra Smith, poetry editor & book designer
Sharon Zetter, poetry editor & book designer
Liza Flum, poetry editor
Matthew Bowie, poetry editor
Jason Bayani, poetry editor
Juliana Paslay, fiction editor
Gail Aronson, fiction editor
Izabella Santana, fiction editor & marketing assistant
Laura Joakimson, marketing assistant specializing in Instagram & Facebook
Ashley Pattison-Scott, executive assistant & *Omniverse* writer
Ariana Nevarez, marketing assistant & *Omniverse* writer
SD Sumner, copyeditor